SAY YES
TO IT

SAY YES TO IT

ELISABETH KÜBLER-ROSS, M.D.

EDITED BY GÖRAN GRIP, M.D.

STATION HILL OPENINGS

BARRYTOWN, LTD.

Published under the Station Hill Openings imprint by Barrytown, Ltd., Barrytown, N.Y. 12507.

Distributed by Consortium Book Sales & Distribution, Inc. 1045 Westgate Drive, Saint Paul, MN 55114-1065.

Text and cover design by Susan Quasha.

The talk in this book has been excerpted from *Death is Of Vital Importance*, Copyright by Elisabeth Kübler-Ross, Station Hill Press, 1995.

A Swedish version of *Death is Of Vital Importance* has been published by Bokförlaget Natur och Kultur under the title *Döden är livsviktig: Om livet, döden och livet efter döden*, Copyright 1991 by Elisabeth Kübler-Ross.

Library of Congress Cataloging-in-Publication Data

Kübler-Ross, Elisabeth.
   Say yes to it / Elisabeth Kübler-Ross ; edited by Göran Grip.
       p.   cm. – (Kübler-Ross in person)
   Excerpted from: Death is of vital importance, 1995.
   ISBN 1-886449-27-9 (lg. Print)
   1. Death.   2. Life.   3. Future life.   4. Spiritual life.
I. Grip, Göran.   II. Title.   III. Series: Kübler-Ross, Elisabeth. Kübler-Ross in person.
[BD444.K797   1997]
155.9'37—dc21   96-48973
                                                              CIP

Printed in the United States of America

CONTENTS

About This Book

Elisabeth Kübler-Ross' words, spoken at the spur of the moment, have been slightly edited here with the aim of creating a readable text. We have taken pains, however, to preserve the quality of immediate presence that is characterized by the author's special magnetism, the power of direct address to a live audience for which she is renowned. We think there is a special meaning in presenting Elisabeth Kübler-Ross "live" on the subject of death and dying — and that this is a key to her message.

This book has been adapted from Elisabeth Kübler-Ross' tape-recorded lecture, *The ARE Lecture*, delivered at the Edgar Cayce Foundation, Virginia Beach, Virginia in 1985.

SAY YES TO IT

Good Friday

Seven years ago to the day I was here the last time. And to me it is very significant. Seven is a very significant number anyway. And Easter is the most important day in our lives — whether you know it or not.

Seven years ago I was here, talking to a group of people. I didn't know then that I was seven years ahead of my heavenly schedule. It didn't work out. And I am very glad that I didn't know seven years ago what was coming. Because then I would have hung myself on the next Christmas tree *(laughter from audience)*.

Every day in my life — and that to me is what Good Friday is all about — Good Friday is viewed by many people as a sad day because of the crucifixion. But without the crucifixion we wouldn't have had the resurrection. And without the windstorms in life my patients would not die with peace and dignity and really knowing what we all need to know at the moment of our death. And so, today I want to talk mainly about the windstorms of life, the purpose of the windstorms of life, and how you should raise your children so they are not afraid of living or of dying.

I'm *not* the "death and dying lady." I hope in the next fifty years I will be known as the "life and living lady"! Because if you live right you will never, ever be afraid to die. *Dying is the greatest pleasure that awaits you.* You should never be worried about that. Instead you should be worried about what you do today. If today you take your highest choice in everything, not just in your deeds but also in your words and your thoughts, then you will have a most incredibly blissful moment at the moment of your death.

All we need to learn is how to raise one generation of youngsters with real unconditional love and firm consistent discipline. There is an old saying somewhere in the Bible — and I never quote that right but you know what I am talking about — the father's sins will be passed on to his children and children's children. That simply means that if you were beaten or if you were sexually abused as a child — a minimum of twenty-five percent of our population grow up with incest — if you were beaten as a kid then you, in your turn, will beat *your* children, because of all the anguish and frustration and the impotent rage which is still inside of you. And if you are not helped to get all this pain out before you are grownups and have your own kids, you will pass this on to the next generation. So I think it is our generation's duty to practice what was taught two thousand years ago: Love thy neighbor as thyself!

And we have to start with ourselves because we cannot love others if we don't love ourselves. And we can never trust others if we cannot trust ourselves. So when I talk about how to raise the next generation, I mean that we have to begin with ourselves, and then it becomes easier and easier and easier.

God created man with five natural emotions. Learn to respect those five natural emotions and don't turn them into unnatural emotions. It is these unnatural emotions which later give you all your unfinished business.

Anger is a natural, God-given gift that, in its natural form, takes fifteen seconds. Fifteen seconds is enough time to say, "No thank you."

And if children are not allowed to express their own assertiveness and authority and natural anger they will end up as Hitlers, small or big Hitlers, full of rage and revenge and hate. The world is full of them.

Grief is a natural emotion which helps you to take care of all the losses in life. How many of you were allowed to cry as little children? If you have a Swiss mother who is very neat and clean and your security blanket gets a little washed out and she says: "Shame!" and she throws it out, it is a horrible loss for a little child. And if you are not allowed to cry or if you are told, "If you don't stop cry-ing I will give you something to cry about, that will shut you up very fast," then you'll rather be quiet than get a spanking. And then, when you grow up, you will have lots of problems with self-pity. You will literally marinate in self-pity. You will not be good at hospice work or helping anybody. You will have lots of shame and guilt.

When you go and watch films like "E.T.," you can see all this shame and guilt by watching the audience. When the light comes on during the break, a lot of people clean their glasses explaining it away by saying that they have become foggy. And that is because they are ashamed to admit that they have cried. This is unfinished business: *you fear that you are not allowed to grieve.*

Love is unconditional. Love has no claims, no expectations. It just *is.*

One form of natural love is holding and hugging the baby, who then feels nurtured and cared for. Another form of love is to be able to say "No." And that is very hard for a lot of people. If you can say to a boy, "I'm not gonna tie your shoe laces. I have all the confidence in the world that you can do that on your own," then he might have a temper tantrum or he might really try to manipulate you. Then you will have to *stick* to it and to convey to him, "I trust that you can do it by yourself. I trust that you can do it even better than I did it at your age." Then he will bend down and try his best, and he will be *so* proud when he finds out that he can learn how to tie his shoelaces himself.

This develops self-trust and self-love. It is very, very important that you know this and if you have any unfinished business, get rid of it, because if you don't, it will not only bug you for the rest of your life, but it will grow like a tapeworm and will eventually suffocate you internally.

When you lose somebody and you have lived fully, you will have no grief *work* whatsoever. You will have a lot of *grief*, but no grief *work*.

Grief *work* is *unfinished business*. It is fear, shame and guilt and all unnatural emotions, and all unfinished business, and all this will naturally drain your energy and decrease your sense of wholeness and health.

Suicide Out of Free Choice

You and you alone are responsible for your choices. But by making the choice you also have to accept the responsibility. Say that someone wants to take his life. When he makes that decision, then he also has to accept the consequences of his choices. And that means he is going to put a *lot* of guilt on his relatives, and a lot of "Why did it happen?" and "What did I do wrong?" and "Why didn't I pick up the cues?" and, you know, all the things that make this situation into a nightmare. And *he* will be responsible for putting *them* through the nightmare. And that is his... load, that he has to bring with him to the other side.

So any time you make a choice, make sure you have the right to make a free choice. It is man's biggest gift that we were given at birth as human beings. We are the only creatures in the Universe, as far as we know, who have been given free choice. But with that goes also a *lot* of responsibility.

And then you really have to differentiate. I would say probably seventy percent of all young people who commit suicide are the physician's responsibility, and that is the only way I can put it: Do we have any psychiatrists in this group? Yes!

Because we really do have to diagnose beginning episodes of undiagnosed manic depressives. We do not diagnose that enough. If a young person is very depressed —well maybe she has lost her boyfriend or she has had a fight or a struggle with her father or mother — we regard that as normal. We do not detect early signs of very, very frequent undiagnosed manic depressives. And the only thing that those patients would need is to be put on Lithium. Lithium is the only thing that I know that is working with these patients. It can take the edge off the depression. They will *still* get depressed but they will reach a certain bottom line and then not go any further. And if they go high, they will still go high but not too high, which they do when they are totally out of control.

And so we have to educate the population much, much more about first episodes of manic depressive psychosis and put the patients on the right medication. I am not a psychiatrist that puts people on lots of drugs. Lithium is one of the few drugs that I use.

It is a very different issue in terms of the consequences of choices if, for example, a young girl commits suicide because of a boyfriend or a mother and she is just furious, "How dare you do that to me? *I* am going to make you so guilty you will be sorry for the rest of your life." Then she commits suicide as an act of revenge, to make somebody else feel *really* guilty. And she pays with her life — she is so furious she would do anything to make the boyfriend feel awful, as an example of how he made *her* feel. This reason for committing suicide has very, very different consequences than if somebody is an undiagnosed manic depressive and is so depressed that no matter what you say or do, she wants nothing else but to end her life. And no matter what you say, you cannot get her out of it.

Suicide as a Result of an Endogenous Depression

How many of you have once felt really, really hopelessly depressed? Then you know what it is like. If you multiply this by ten, then you will know what a manic-depressive feels in his or her depression. Nothing makes any sense, nothing! It's... it's worse than nothing. It's total vacuum. There is absolutely no way of getting out into the sunshine. And for the depressed person, the only solution is to end it all like this, because it has become unbearable.

You understand that at the end, when you do the life review after you die, that will be evaluated as if you had died of cancer. That form of depression and suicide is an illness that you are not held responsible for.

You cannot "graduate" until you have learned all the lessons that you came to learn in this life time, and also until you have taught the things that you came to teach. Life is nothing but a school, literally a school where you are tested, where you have to pass your tests. And if you pass your tests you get a double whopper. If you pass that next test, which is much tougher than the first one, then you get a triple whopper. And it goes on and on and on, but it doesn't get easier. It gets worse! It gets harder and tougher each time, but it also *comes* easier. Do you understand what I mean? It is like giving math problems for a fifth grader to a first grader: it would be impossible for him. But to give those problems to a fifth grader is a different thing. By fifth grade he is already better prepared and he will have a fair chance to make it.

When you think that you have really made it to the top of the mountain, and that you can really take it now, then you get the two-by-four over you head *(knowing laughter from audience)*. If you get the two-by-four over your head and you survive, then you get... I don't know what's the next size to a two-by-four? But you get a big stick over your head. How many of you have gone through at least a two-by-four stage? *(Answer from audience, "I think that I have done that.")* Did you think that it was tough? *("Yes!")* Well, then the best is yet to come! *(laughter from audience)*

That's what life is all about. The sole purpose of life is spiritual evolution: to grow until you are so perfect that they can put you through a tumbler. And you know that when you are put into that tumbler of life, which is symbolically speaking, your choice — and *nobody else's* choice — you come out either crushed or polished.

The Difference Between Rescue and Help

When you accomplish somebody's rescue you are not helping. You all understand that on some level. Because if you rescue someone you make *him* weak and *you* will be the bigshot. If you rescue him and Band-Aid him, you don't help him at all.

We are all our brother's keepers and our sister's keepers. We are responsible to help wherever it is needed. But you have to know the difference between *rescuing* somebody: trying to fix something in somebody else's life, and *helping* him: to be available when that person has learned to be humble enough to ask for help. It is a very thin line between being a rescuer and being a real helper, a decent human being.

(Someone in the audience asks Elisabeth what to do when somebody who is very ill says that he doesn't want to live anymore.) Did anyone talk to you about the universal laws? You need to know some very basic universal laws. *Thou shalt not kill* is an absolute universal law, and that goes for all mankind. It is not only for our own religion but for every single one of them.

If somebody asks you to kill him, no matter for what reason, you first have to find out why he doesn't want to live anymore. How many of you are taking care of people who don't want to live, who are tied down to a chair, incontinent, who stare into space, and nobody kisses them or touches them?

How many of you would like to exist that way? Nobody, of course. If you know... if you can really identify with that person, "I wouldn't like to exist that way," then ask yourself, "What can I do to change his situation so that he can not only exist until he dies, but can really live until he dies?" Then you go about changing this or that for him.

How many of you have seen Katie's film that we made about dancing with old people who were all paralyzed and in wheel chairs? You have not seen it?

We have a video tape we made on how to help old people — and on purpose you pick *very* old people, not sixty-two year olds, so we don't have to think that they could be us (*laughter from audience*). You take a group of eighty- to one-hundred-and-four-year-old women and men in a nursing home who are all paralyzed and in wheel chairs. And typically very old, a very helpless kind of not very peppy old people — and try to teach them how to live.

We got this dancer who showed them how to dance. And they were all paralyzed you understand, and in wheel chairs. So she put the wheel chairs in a circle and we had a photographer who took a video of what we were doing with those people. But he didn't do it like we would do it, where the people show off in front of the camera, smiling and trying to look sweet and happy. No, he had the camera behind them and he just photographed their feet, dead feet, just hanging there. And then as she danced — and she used Tchaikovsky and Mozart and all the old classical music — you suddenly began to see the foot moving *(amazement from audience)*. And then you see, they are really going. And you saw an old man just bounce, starting to fiddle around with the woman next to him *(big laughter from audience)* and started to grab and started to touch. And things were happening, and on this film you can see all this.

And the old man got engaged to that old lady later on *(happy laughter)*. And she insisted that she would be his bride, but she only wanted to be his bride because she wanted a new dress! *(laughter)* I mean, a shrewd old lady *(big laughter)*.

You should see this film. And you should see this nursing home. *(Question from audience, "What is the name of that nursing home?")* I have had a stroke, I have no more memory. But the video tape is in the news letter. Something about dancing with old ladies. And they dance like you wouldn't believe it. And all with one person who plays the right music and brings life into that life.

My Mother

When my mother was old she had one really big hang-up: she could not receive. She would give her shirt away; she could do anything for anybody. She worked her butt off all her life. She raised triplets and a six-year-old boy and you know what it was like sixty years ago to raise triplets. You didn't have a laundry machine, you didn't have Pampers, you didn't have hot water. She had to nurse us for nine months every three hours day and night and it was tough. But she gave and she gave and she was all love.

But she could not take anything. She could not do that. I mean she was pathological!

If a neighbor would bake a pie on Saturday and bring it to her just to give her a break and have some dessert ready, the next weekend she had to bake a pie and bring back to her neighbor.

Do you know people like this? Would you please tell them my story so they don't end up the same way? I myself have to learn the same thing.

She was terribly afraid that one day she would end up as a vegetable because she would then be *totally doomed* to receive. That was absolutely the worst thing that could ever happen in her life. And we always pulled her leg and said, "You are going to be sorry if you can't just gracefully accept it. You make this woman happy by accepting the pie." But she couldn't hear.

She was afraid of becoming a vegetable, and one day we got a phone call saying that Mama had been found in the bathroom with a massive stroke. She was paralyzed, unable to speak, unable to move anything, unable to do anything.

We rushed her to the hospital. The only part she was able to move was her left hand a little bit. And because she tried to use her left hand to pull the tube out of her nose — she needed that tube naturally — they tied that hand down, and that one became totally useless too. So she couldn't move one-tenth of an inch of her body. And I promised her, "I'll help you to live until you die."

But I could not help her to die. Already, sometime *before* the stroke, she begged me to give her something if she ever became a vegetable. And I said, "I can't do that.

How can I do that to a mother who kept me alive by nursing me every three hours, day and night, with all the sacrifice, and now I should.... Really, I can't do that." She was furious with me.

I made a mistake then — she was in her full senses — when I said, "I can't help you to die but I will help you to live until you die." I knew that she was pissed at me and not happy and could not understand and she said, "You are the only doctor in the family, it would be very easy."

I did not buy it, thank God, and I am a softy.

Three days after this discussion I was back in America and got the phone call from home that she had been found with a massive stroke. I immediately returned to Switzerland.

We rushed her to the hospital where they had a respirator ready and the whole works. And she used — you know now what the rubber hose is,[1] right? — she

---

[1] In Elisabeth's workshops the participants learn to beat a mattress with a piece of rubber hose in order to facilitate the expression of pain, rage and impotence.

used the aluminum side rail as her rubber hose.

She rattled that aluminum side rail so you could hear it outside the hospital. When you came in you could hear the rattle and the rage. You know, she couldn't speak, so this was her only way of expressing herself. I knew that I couldn't stand listening to that sound although I understood her rage. She was totally impotent and she just had to let people wash her, feed her, take care of everything for her.

And so I asked her if she wanted me to take her to the equivalent of a hospice. This was a long time ago when they didn't have hospices. But what I had in mind was an old... it's like where nuns take care of patients and just love them. No machines, no respirators, no nothing. And she said yes, she would like that. That was her real, clear message.

In Switzerland, it's very hard to find decent places like that because you have a waiting list for two or three years. And that was the only time when I was grateful that I was a triplet, that we were three people who could put our heads together to find a place for her. One of my sisters is *very* seductive, the other one is a real politician, and I came from America, which means I have money *(laughter from audience)*. This was a long time ago when a dollar was one to four.

I was supposed to pay for whatever it cost, my seductive sister was going to try to seduce the doctor *(laughter)* to give her a bed, and the politician was allowed to use any dirty tricks *(laughter)*. Who do you think got the bed within forty-eight hours? *(Answer from audience, "The dollar?")*

Not in *Switzerland*, thank God *(big laughter)*. The seductive one! *(Amazement from audience)* In forty-eight hours she had a bed! We never asked her how she did it *(very big laughter)*.

She got a bed in Basel. I had my mother in Zurich, which is, you know quite far away, and she got the bed from somebody who had just died and they just swapped the beds, got it fast.

The trip from Zurich to Basel with my mother was the best trip with any critically ill patient I've ever made in my entire life. Before the trip I had to empty her house. You know what it is like to give away anything and everything that belongs to your mother? *(with the slightest catch in her voice)* And she was still alive, but you know she can never again move into... Pictures, books, clothes, absolutely everything. This was *my* last home too, you know, so I also gave up a chance to go back home, whatever that was.

I made a list of all the things that she was attached to a little bit, like... one day we had bought her a little mink hat, the next Christmas we bought her the collar, you know. We all saved money to buy this mink hat and collar. She was so proud that she had the little mink hat, for my mother is a very modest woman.

I made a list of all those things and I rented an ambulance to take me and her from Zurich to Basel. I also bought a bottle of eggnog —spiced eggnog which is called "Ei-congnac." It is more cognac than eggs *(laughter from audience)*. I don't think you have it here. It is a delicious Dutch drink. You don't know that it is booze but you *feel* it *(laughter from audience)*. None of us in the family ever drank alcohol but now I needed a bottle of egg cognac.

I and my mother went to Basel in the ambulance. I had this master list of all her things that I needed to find a home for, you know, all the things she loved. And I told her that she must make [the sound] "hrrr" when I found the right person for the right thing.

For each and every one of her things on my list I went through all the possible candidates, like the wife of the mailman and the wife of the milkman. I mentioned a name and nothing happened, and I mentioned another name and still nothing happened, and I mentioned another name and then every time I mentioned the right person she suddenly made, "Hrrr," and then I wrote down next to the hat or the collar who was to have it. And every time we hit the nail on the head we... *(demonstrates how they took a sip of egg cognac)* we had a drink *(laughter from audience)*. And by the time we arrived in Basel the bottle was empty, but *(with laughter in her voice)* the *list* was complete. That was my last finishing of unfinished business with my Mama and it was the most joyful trip I've ever had with any patient in my life.

But then she got into this hospital, which was like a two hundred years old building, and the side rails were made of hardwood and you could not move them!

In the hospital in Basel we took her "rattle" away. You know, that was her toy, her only way of expressing her rage and impotence. And *I* said, "Well, that's only gonna last for few days, and she's gonna stick it out until then."

But she *existed* this way for four years. Four years! No sound. No way to express herself. And she stared at me and I felt guilty, and she had a knack for making me feel guilty just by her looks.

I was furious with God. I cannot tell you, I could have shred Him to pieces if

I'd had the chance. I used every language, Swiss, French, Italian, English, everything. He didn't budge. He gave no response. No *nothing*.

And I said to Him, "You S.O.B." *(in an angry voice)* in *our* language. And I got absolutely no reaction from Him. That made me even more furious.

You know, you can call Him every name, and He just sits there and loves you. *(She growls in mock anger. Laughter from audience)*. You know, it is like when you are really mad and somebody says, "Sweetie Pie" to you *(laughter from audience)*. And you could kill Him. But He is *dead* already. You can't even kill Him. And I went through all the rage, the bargaining, the depression and the guilt trip and the whole works.

This rage of mine lasted not only for the four years that she continued *existing* in that body, but weeks and months after she died I still tried to review my opinion of God. I really needed to come to grips with this. I thought, "He can't be such an S.O.B. But how can a loving, compassionate, understanding God let this woman suffer who has been seventy-nine years loving and giving and caring and sharing?" I mean, that is not God. That's the other one, and I don't want to have anything to do with him, that was my opinion.

⚜

And then, months after she died — needless to say we were very relieved and glad when she finally died — I took the... I don't know how to say it, but one day I reviewed my opinion of God. And the moment I realized what this was all about I almost jumped out of my skin. And I said, "Thank you, thank you, thank you, thank you, you are the most generous man that ever existed." And I had a thing about cheap men *(laughter from audience)*. Cheap men were my hang-up in my first workshop. So to call Him a generous man was the biggest compliment I could give God *(laughter)* and it had to be a man, not a woman, because I had a hang-up with cheap men, not with cheap women. So when I *finally* did this review I jumped out of my skin, and I said, "You are the most generous man that has ever existed."

You know, what suddenly came to me on that day is that you get your lessons one way or another, you understand, and *you* yourself are responsible for what lessons you *get* — and, since I at least *knew* this, I shouldn't have had such a tough one — and at last I realized what He did for her, and that you are only able to see that from a distance. So when you sit on top, when you sit at your brother's side, you are *so* nonobjective that you cannot see. But if you go to Timbuktu or you go into the wilderness and meditate or you go to Arizona and away or whatever you do.... It takes distance to see clearly.

And with my distance from my horribly suffering mother who laid guilt trips on me with her looks, I finally saw that this is the most generous God because he allowed her to give and give and give and love for seventy-nine years and she only had to learn to receive for four years.

You understand that? Generous —

Nowadays if I see somebody who just has to learn it the hard way because he didn't learn it the easy way, I know for sure it's *His* doing. But we are not taught that. But you see, we were taught this earlier, and then we really knew that we, ourselves, are responsible for whatever we don't hear, cannot hear. This is what I meant before; you get a two-by-four over your head. If you don't acknowledge the two-by-four, then the next time you will get an even bigger stick over your head, which might even break your skull.

❦

For about a year I was taught by my students that I had to relax, I had to learn R & R. I didn't know what R & R was. It doesn't exist in my vocabulary. No matter how often I asked, I was told that R & R meant Rest and Relaxation. Two minutes later I forgot and I kept going and going and going and didn't.

The last time I asked I was told, "You really have to relax now. Take a step out, you can't do everything, but you have to learn to rest. You cannot go on like this seventeen hours a day, seven days a week." And, yeah, I heard it, sure, and I thought to myself that when I got around to it, I would do it.

Then in August 1988 I had my stroke and I was paralyzed, and I couldn't speak.

In the beginning of December 1988, I was told that if I didn't *really* practice R & R now, I would get another... "popra" I think they called it... it's a little stroke.

If you don't learn from the first lesson, they just give you another one and a tougher one to that. So now I'm practicing R & R and this is my first workshop in ages, where I just sit in for a little while.

Now, *if* I had given my mother an overdose — to answer your question — my mother *would* have had to come back, would have had to start from scratch, and learn to receive. Maybe she would have had to be born with a spina bifida, or to be born paralyzed, or incontinent or something, so that somebody would have had to clean her "tusch"... what do you call that? Clean her...? And maybe they would also have had to feed her and do *everything* for her, so that she would be *forced* to learn to receive.

Now, by saying "NO," because I really loved her — I still do — she was spared a whole lifetime of agony. Do you understand what I mean by that?

You cannot *rescue* people, because if you do that, they will still have to learn the lesson that you rescued them from. And this is for the same reason that you cannot go into a high school exam and take somebody else's tests to get an ECFMG if you are in medical school, or a high school diploma for somebody else. They have to make it themselves. Love, real love is the answer. My teachers give me the best definition of what love is really all about — real love means that you allow them to learn their own lessons without rescuing them. Love is to know when to put training wheels on the child's bicycle and also to know when to take them off. That is love. Removing the training wheels is much more difficult than putting them on, and yet eventually you will *have* to remove them.

So if someone wants to be rescued — in this sense of the word — lovingly tell him that whatever he learns from this agony, *he* picked it in order to pass his tests, and if you fake it and make it easy for him, then you cheat him out of a quantum leap of progress and he will hate you for God knows how long for taking his last chance away to learn that particular lesson.

Do you all understand that? It is a very thin line between being a *rescuer* and being a real *helper*, a decent human being. It is very important that you understand this.

(A woman in the audience thinks that Elisabeth contradicts herself when she says that you should refrain from rescuing someone who is in a difficult situation and asks for help.)

No, you *are* allowed to go as far as to deplete your resources: if I meet somebody who has lots of pain from cancer, I

put him on a painkiller. If I meet somebody whom I can verify as having an undiagnosed manic-depressive psychosis, I
naturally put him on Lithium. That is as
far as you're allowed to go as healthcare
people. There *is* a limit to what you can
gratify in terms of what they ask of you.
Real love is to say, "No thank you. This is
as much as I can do for you. And the rest,
you have to do on your own."

Yes, it's difficult, it's not easy. There are
lots of times when I don't know if it's
decent to even prolong somebody's life.
Maybe they will not be able to have any
function at all in life and, as a physician,
I was trained to use all the life support-
ing machines there are. And then I know
that if this were me I wouldn't want that
to happen. But here in America you have
lawsuits. You are obliged to do it.

Number two: if there is a family mem-
ber who gives you the evil eye, saying
you haven't tried this and that, then you
will have to decide whether you are going to gratify the patient's real needs or
whether you are going to take care of that

one relative who has so much unfinished business with the patient that *he* can't let him go. It is not all black and white. It is not easy at all.

Active euthanasia, in my opinionated opinion, is a one-hundred-and-fifty percent NO. Because you do not know why people have to go through that particular lesson. And if you try to rescue them, you will be cursed. Do you understand what I mean? It's very important.

(Question from audience, "Could you explain how getting rid of your unfinished business helps you grow spiritually?") To me it's the only way. How much time do you have? *(laughter from audience)* I will tell you briefly how I got rid of my Hitler if you don't mind. It will take at least fifteen minutes.

My Father

You have to become honest. That is the absolutely basic requirement. You cannot be a phony-baloney. And I don't mean with other people but with yourself. When you get ugly, negative, angry, hateful, anything icky, then acknowledge that it is *your* stuff and not your fellow man's.

You know, I give workshops all over the world to help people get rid of their unfinished business. Years ago I was asked to go to Hawaii to give a workshop. We always look for some old convents because they have big space, a gorgeous environment, most of them are empty, they are not too expensive, and the food is halfway decent. These are our basic requirements. And also, naturally, when you scream, that the cops don't come. So it has to be really remote.

And we couldn't find a place in Hawaii. We were almost ready to give up the whole thing when a woman called me up and said, "Dr. Ross, we have just the ideal place. The only problem is that we can only give it to you sometime in April next year." I'm always booked two years ahead of time, so that didn't bother me. I've also had so many incredible experiences that I know that I am always at the right time at the right place. So why bother about the details? Right? *(laughter from audience)*

So I didn't bother about those details. I have gotten into a lot of trouble because of that too. But anyhow I said, "Yes, fine, we will take it." And I sent a check for one thousand dollars and I forgot about it.

About a year and a half later it became time to get the plane ticket to the right island and I had to look into the details. And when I got the letter with the details on the time and the place and the date I had a total temper tantrum. I was so ugly and icky you would not believe it. I mean it lasted more than fifteen seconds. It was more like fifteen days (*laughter from audience*).

I mean I was uglier than I remember having been since I was two years old having temper tantrums. When your emotional quadrant overreacts, your intellectual quadrant comes to your rescue immediately. Because you could never acknowledge that this is you. So my head immediately said to me, "Those jerks! They gave me Easter week! Easter week for one of my workshops, that's impossible!" And I blamed *them* for giving me

Easter week. I said to myself, "You know, I have kids at home and I'm traveling too much already, and I don't see enough of them. Next time *they* will take not only Easter away, but *they* are gonna take Christmas away. Why am I a mother at all, I never see my kids, and it's all because of *them!*"

Then I thought, "That's ridiculous. I can paint Easter eggs the weekend before, or the weekend after, so it can't be *that* terrible."

But my next line of defense was, "No, Easter will be terrible for a workshop because you don't get any Catholics. You also don't get any good Jews because it's Passover at the same time. And to have a workshop with only Protestants, I can't *stand* that." *(laughter and applause from audience)* I actually mean this very seriously because to me the beauty of my workshops is that you get every race, every creed, every age from eleven-year-old dying children to one hundred and four year old ladies. And if you have only one kind, you don't learn that we are all the same, that we all come from the same source and return to the same source.

I had so many excuses, but I don't want to trouble you with all of them. I was very *good*. I mean, I am a psychiatrist. I came up with *very* good excuses for being angry, you have no idea!

And nothing worked! Nothing!

I flew to Hawaii, the biggest sourpuss you have ever seen. I was even mad at my neighbors in the plane for drinking and for all sorts of stuff. I mean, I was just icky.

When I saw the place they gave me and that they assigned me to my room — it was a residential school for girls — I had another temper tantrum. I almost killed the guy who gave me the key to the room. And you have to understand why I was overreacting. I was born a triplet. It's a nightmare to be a triplet, because in those days you know, we had the same shoes, the same dresses, the same clothes, the same ribbons, the same grade cards because the teachers didn't know who was who, and so they gave us all straight C's *(laughter)*.

We even had identical night pots. And we had to pee at the same time *(laughter)* and we weren't allowed to get up from the dinner table until all three had finished *(laughter)*. So that's a big blessing I know now, and without it, no doubt I would not have made it. Because when I became a public commodity later on I was able to lecture to two or three thousand people in New York, and then sign three hundred books, then dash to Kennedy airport and just make it to the plane, and then I just *had* to go to the bathroom. I dashed in quickly and the minute I sat down, a hand came onto the door with a book, "Could you sign?" *(big laughter from audience)*

You understand why I had to be raised as a triplet! It was a preparation for my life's work.

So if you, like me, never, ever, ever had any private space, you become very tuned in to the needs of other people for *their* private space. As I walked into this room in the residential school for girls I knew that this... (I called him a crook)... this crook sent all these children home for Easter week so he could rent out the rooms and make ten thousand dollars. To make money I can understand, but what I could absolutely not forgive this guy for was that he didn't tell the girls that other people were going to live in their rooms. And any mother knows that kids don't leave certain things on the table if they know that somebody else is going to live there, right?

So it was for me like entering the sacred, private space of a child. And I really felt I couldn't use their bed or use their space. I was *angry* as can be.

Then this man made the mistake of inviting himself to my workshop. And I hated him so much I couldn't say "No." Then at dinner he stood at the end of the table where *my* group ate, and he said with a sweet smile, "Your group eats too much." And you know what I did? Me, a teacher of unconditional love? I went to every workshop participant and said, "Wouldn't you like to finish this spaghetti? How about eating the last meatballs? We don't want to leave anything. Let's finish this salad! Here is one more biscuit!" It was like an obsession. I could not leave the table as long as there was one bread crumb on the table. That was my revenge *(laughter from audience)*.

But you understand, I didn't know that at the time. I was compelled, "I'm gonna show this guy that *my* group can eat." And those who ate four times, I loved them four times more than those who ate small courses. I did feel ugly but I couldn't stop it. I could not stop it as long as there was any food left on the table.

And then at night we did the drawing test. We gave the people a piece of paper and a box of Crayola. This guy very casually said, "Ten cents for a sheet of paper." This is a school! Sixty-nine cents for the *use* of a box of Crayola. Twenty-five cents for each cup of coffee. This went on all week long. Five cents, twenty-five cents, seventeen cents.

By Wednesday we sat in my workshop, and I was teaching unconditional love. But I couldn't look at this guy, because then something would have happened *(laughter from audience)*. And I was so drained you have no idea. I was exhausted trying to keep the lid on. And I didn't know what was happening.

Later, on Wednesday, I realized that I really was fantasizing that I would like to put that guy through a meat slicer *(laughter from audience)*.

By Thursday, I wanted to put iodine on every slice *(laughter from audience)*. And by Friday, I cannot remember what it was, but it was ugly too.

So Friday, at noon, I left the workshop. The workshop was a success except that *I* was ruined. I had not an inch of energy left. And normally I work seven days a week seventeen hours a day and I am very peppy.

I knew that somebody that I wasn't aware of pushed the button for Hitler within me. I had never felt so dirty, ugly, mean, nasty, like you cannot believe it.

So I left that place fast before there was a homicide *(laughter from audience)*.

As I walked onto the plane I could barely make the steps. I was physically so exhausted. I first went to California, where I was to meet my friends, and then I planned to move on to Chicago hopefully to have a lovely Easter Sunday. In the plane all the way to California I was trying to think my head off, "What did this guy push, what kind of a button did he push in me?"

By the time we landed in California I suddenly became aware that I am very allergic to cheap men *(reluctant laughter from audience)*. By "cheap men" I mean what you call a "penny-pincher." For I was now fully aware that if he would have been honest enough to say, "We need another two thousand dollars. We underestimated the costs," then I would have written a check for him. But the smaller the amount, the more likely I was to kill him.

I didn't know where it all came from. I had no idea.

Anybody who wants to work for Shanti Nilaya is asked to make two commitments. One is that he or she makes his house calls and his work with patients free of charge, so that he never can charge a penny. And the other commitment, which is more difficult to fulfill, is that each time he gets in touch with Hitler within, he has to work on it until he gets rid of it. Of course no one can go around preaching something and not practicing it. So now I knew I had to get rid of whatever it was.

We also have a rule that you can never ever ask anybody for something more than three times. The reason for this is that if you ask someone for something more than three times you deprive him of free choice. And it has to be *his* choice if what you ask for is to be given freely.

So now when I was going to meet my friends in California, I thought maybe I would get away with three questions about the workshop. And I came there and they said, "How was the workshop?" I said, "FINE."

"How was your workshop?" they asked again, catching my harsh tone of voice. I added two more words before the "fine" and it sounded very ugly. The third time they asked they did the worst thing that anybody can do to someone who is really ugly, and that is to be sweet with her. They put their hands on my head and in the *sweetest* way they said, "Tell us all about Easter bunnies."

And I totally exploded. I said, "Easter bunnies! You must be kidding. I'm fifty years old. I'm a physician. I'm a psychiatrist. I don't believe in Easter bunnies anymore." I made this incredible speech and at the end I said, "If you want to talk to your clients that way you know *that's* your choice, but *not* to me." And the minute I said "not to me" I started to sob and cry and I cried for eight hours.

And my whole pool of unfinished business, repressed for almost half a century, came out and out and out like an unending kind of an ocean. And as I shared the pain and the anguish and the tears and the agony and the unfairness, the memory followed, the way it always does after you have emptied your pool. As I got my emotions out — my bottled-up emotions — the memory came when I was very, very little:

My identical sister was forever on my father's lap. My other sister was forever on my mother's lap. There was no third lap left. I must have waited for God knows how long for one of them to pick me up. And as they never picked me up and never took me on their lap I began to reject *them* because I couldn't tolerate the situation otherwise. And I became a very arrogant two-year-old who said, "I don't need *you*. Don't touch me." Like I'm independent.

My love objects became bunnies. I had rabbits. And I know now that they were the only living creatures that knew me from my sister, because I fed them and they always came when I went there. I loved them beyond anything. I am sure that people could be raised by animals. I am absolutely sure of that.

My problem was that my father was a thrifty Swiss. They are all thrifty but not cheap. I hope you understand the difference *(laughter from audience)*.

Every six months he had the desire to have a roast. He could have afforded *any* roast, but *he* desired to have a rabbit roast. They were very authoritarian fifty years ago, and so he ordered me to pick one of my love objects to bring it to the butcher. And *I* had to pick — you know, like an executioner — pick a rabbit, which one's turn was it? I had to pick one of my rabbits and I had to carry him down the mountains for half an hour to the butcher. It was a tortuous thing to do. Then I had to deliver him to the butcher and after a while he always came out with a paper bag with the warm meat in it. I had to carry the meat back up the hill for half an hour and deliver it to my mother's kitchen. Later I had to sit at the dining room table and watch my family eat my beloved bunny.

Because I was an arrogant little child who covered up my insecurity and my inferiority with arrogance, I was darned careful not to let them know how much they hurt me. You understand, "If you don't love me I will also not tell you how much this hurts me." I never spoke up. I never cried. I *never* shared with a human being my pain and my anguish and my torture. I held it all inside.

It took about six months to recover and by then it was time for the next bunny.

Well, in my regressed state, when all these memories came and the tears were rolling, I became six and a half again and remembered like it was yesterday how I was kneeling down in the grass talking to my last bunny who also was my most beloved one. He was called Blackie. He was pitch black and absolutely gorgeous and very well fed with young dandelion leafs. I begged him to run away but he loved me so much he didn't move. And so eventually I had to bring him to the butcher.

I went there and handed Blackie over to him. After awhile he came out again with the paper bag and said. "Damned shame you had to bring this rabbit. In a day or two she would have had little bunnies." I didn't know it was a she-bunny.

I walked home like a robot. I never had rabbits again. I never ever shared my pain and my anguish.

Today — as a psychiatrist — I understand that after that last bunny was sacrificed I had to keep the lid on not to become aware of all my tears and inner screams. Every time I met a thrifty man I had to put the lid on tighter and tighter and tighter.

Half a century later I ran into that one really thrifty man. And I almost killed him. I don't mean that symbolically speaking. *(laughter from audience; Elisabeth answers):* No, you really have to know. If, on Friday morning, this man had asked me for another nickel he would be dead and I would be in jail *(laughter from audience).* I am *not* meaning that as a joke. I was at the end of my rope, because my defenses were beginning to fall apart.

I thank God that we have this method of externalization used in workshops, because when I poured all this out with my friends in California it made me able to correlate and understand where my allergy to "cheap men" came from. Now I can see a hundred cheap men, and I feel that it is their problem. It's not mine any longer.

Diagnosing Black Bunnies

Out of gratitude for having been in a safe place with people who really were able to help me diagnose my unfinished business, I went back to Hawaii and we asked, in a prison, if we could be given the permission to diagnose the "black bunny" in each one of their prisoners. It took a long time before they trusted us. But eventually we were given permission to do what we wanted. Two years ago the first so-called criminal was discharged into our custody. This man now uses his life pain and anguish to help other young kids not to end up in jail.

When I shared my black bunny story in that prison, an old man asked me, "Are you not afraid to be locked up here with all these criminals?" I said "If you are a criminal I'm a criminal too." And I hope you understand that I really mean that. There is this possibility in all of us.

I told him my black bunny story. And a very, very young man who could have been my son (he didn't even have a beard yet) jumped up and said, "My God, now I know why I ended up in jail."

He shared a very brief story. He said that when he was fourteen and a half, one day when he was in school, he suddenly had this incredible urge that he had to go home. When you have this terrible urge without knowledge from your intellect, it means that it comes from the intuitive quadrant. That tells me already, for a four-teen-and-a-half-year-old boy to have that awareness, that he must have been raised with a lot of love.

And he followed his urge and dashed home. He went into the good living room. Hawaiian kids don't go into the good living room, but he walked straight in there and he saw his dad lying, half sitting on a couch, his face totally gray. He said he had such love for his father that he didn't have to scream, he didn't have to call anybody. He just sat behind him and held his dad in his arms and just loved him.

After about ten minutes he realized that his father had stopped breathing. He said that it was such an incredible moment of peace that he didn't want to go and get somebody, he just wanted to sit there for a little while.

At that moment, the paternal grandmother walked in. She had horrible problems with competition and envy. She screamed and blamed him for causing the death of her son. And he told us, "I just put the lid on. I didn't want to ruin that sacred moment." And so, he did not respond to her accusations.

Three days later, during the Hawaiian funeral, where the whole community and all the family and relatives were, this grandmother again blew her lid and blamed him in public for the death of his father. And again he said, "I just had to keep quiet. I didn't want to ruin my beloved father's funeral."

Two and a half years later he was found outside of a grocery store with a... what do you call those things?... a sawed off shotgun... holding it to the temple of a grouchy, miserable-looking old woman. He just stood there, God knows for how long. After a while he looked at her face and said, "Oh my God, what am I doing here? I don't want to hurt you." He apologized, dropped his gun and ran home.

But in a community, you know, they catch you fast. He was given twenty years in jail.

There are no bad human beings. There is a gorgeous children's book where children write letters to God. One letter says, "God didn't make junk." Do you remember it? Everybody is born perfect. If your physical quadrant is not perfect, you are gifted with a more open spiritual quadrant. Everybody is perfect. And if they are ending up not perfect, it's because they have not experienced enough love and understanding.

So I hope, over Easter, which is a marvelous time to do this kind of work, that you look at your own black bunny, and when you see somebody whom you hate, then try to understand and not judge.

(In a warm, joyful and happy voice): Thank you and have a happy Easter! *(Applause)*